Isabel & Mac.

The Mayor and Mayoress

Margot & Neville

January 1996.

IMPRESSIONS OF WOOLLAHRA

IMPRESSIONS OF WOOLLAHRA

PAST AND PRESENT

Compiled and edited by Elaine Cassidy, Dinah Goddard,
Faye Lawrence, Judy May and June Poland

Introduction by Professor Max Kelly, President, National Trust of Australia (NSW)

Published on behalf of the Woollahra Bicentennial Community Committee
by Allen & Unwin

Sydney   Wellington   London   Boston

First published in 1988
Allen & Unwin Australia Pty Ltd
An Unwin Hyman company
8 Napier Street, North Sydney, NSW 2060 Australia

Allen & Unwin New Zealand Limited
60 Cambridge Terrace, Wellington, New Zealand

Unwin Hyman Limited
15-17 Broadwick Street, London W1V IFP England

Allen & Unwin Inc.
8 Winchester Place, Winchester, Mass 01890 USA

National Library of Australia
Cataloguing-in-Publication entry:

Impressions of Woollahra, past and present.

ISBN 0 04 351071 X.

1. Woollahra (N.S.W) — Description — Views — Exhibitions — 2. Woollahra (N.S.W.) —
History — Exhibitions. 3. Woollahra (N.S.W.) in art — Exhibitions. I. Cassidy, Elaine.
II. Woollahra Bicentennial Community Committee.

994.4'1'0074.

Designed by Deborah Brash/Brash Design
Set in 10 pt. Biblia by Love Computer Typesetting Pty Ltd
Printed by Colorcraft Ltd, Hong Kong

Australia
1788-1988

This publication has been partially funded by
The Australian Bicentennial Authority
to celebrate Australia's Bicentenary in 1988.

CONTENTS

ILLUSTRATIONS

PREFACE

IN 1982, the New South Wales State Government requested that all local shires and councils establish joint community/Council committees to plan for and to celebrate the Bicentenary in 1988. In Woollahra, this request was widely publicised, and a committee of volunteers was formed. Many ideas for projects for the forthcoming celebrations were discussed.

A history sub-committee was appointed, one of whose projects was the organisation and presentation of exhibitions prior to 1988, throughout the municipality. The exhibitions would explore Woollahra's place in the history of the early European settlement of New South Wales, and stimulate community interest in and awareness of the forthcoming Bicentenary. Exhibits were drawn from various sources, both private and public collections. Three exhibitions were held: *Woollahra in Camera* (historic photographs and postcards), *Dear Nell* (postcards), and *Woollahra Reflected: 18th and 19th Century Paintings and Drawings.*

Another project of the Bicentennial Community Committee was an art contest *Impressions of Woollahra* arranged by Mr. Robin Brampton to present a series of images of contemporary Woollahra. The competition was acquisitive, and the winning entries became the property of Woollahra Municipal Council.

The Woollahra Bicentennial Community Committee applied for and received a grant from the New South Wales Council of the Australian Bicentennial Authority to produce a book recording the highlights of the four exhibitions. Subsequently, Elaine Cassidy, Dinah Goddard, Faye Lawrence and June Poland, of the Woollahra Bicentennial Community Committee's history sub-committee, together with the chairman of the Woollahra Bicentennial Community Committee, Judy May, compiled this book.

The committee is grateful to the following persons and organisations for their assistance:

Dinah Dysart, Director of the S.H. Ervin Gallery of the National Trust of Australia (NSW), for assistance in the early stages of the project

The Librarians in the Pictures section of the Mitchell Library, State Library of New South Wales

Woollahra Municipal Council, and reference staff at Woollahra Municipal Library

The New South Wales Government through funding provided by the New South Wales Bicentennial Council

Robert Walker, Photographer, for photographing many of the paintings and prints.

The committee gratefully acknowledges permission to reproduce original paintings, drawings and engravings from:

The Australian National Gallery, Canberra
The Rex Nan Kivell Collection, National Library of Australia, Canberra
The Art Gallery of NSW
The Mitchell Library, State Library of NSW
The Dixson Library, State Library of NSW
The Dixson Galleries, State Library of NSW

Deutscher Fine Art, Victoria
Trevor Bussell Fine Art Gallery, Woollahra
Private collections

and photographs and postcards from:

The Mitchell Library, State Library of NSW
The Historic Photograph Collection, University of Sydney
New South Wales Government Printing Office, Australia
Woollahra Municipal Library
The Josef Lebovic collection
Private collections

INTRODUCTION

THIS BOOK SEEKS TO CREATE the sense of place that is Woollahra. It does so via resort to a diverse array of impressions, visual and literary, that together suggest the mosaic of the region as it has evolved over time. Woollahra is here shown to be a favoured place. Overall there is the water, those magnificent coves and bays of Sydney Harbour that give to the region its one great dominating characteristic. From its consequent cliffs, headlands and valleys, Woollahra looks always north, across a panorama that is frequently sublime, often spectacular. And upon this landscape inhabitants both black and white have inscribed many marks.

One of the most compelling aspects of Woollahra is that the great white fleet of 1788 found this land much as the creator had probably intended. The signs of black occupancy were, by later standards, extraordinarily discreet. Although such discretion was necessarily practical — the need to maintain a balance between inhabitant and the natural environment in order to survive — it was nonetheless a case of environmental man being introduced to industrial man as the First Fleet bobbed past Camp Cove two hundred years ago. Inscribed upon rocks above this cove are markings, thankfully protected, of the first inhabitants of Woollahra.

As Candice Bruce and Anita Callaway reveal, it took many decades for Woollahra to become 'built-up'. Even then, it was almost exclusively the favoured of the Colony who sought to live there. The colonial administrative classes chose wisely, and built well. Campbell Riddell's *Lindesay*, Sir Thomas Mitchell's *Carthona* and W. C. Wentworth's *Vaucluse* are but some of many who began the transformation of a still alien landscape. They were soon to be joined by the merchants of the town who, having made great wealth, sought to establish households of almost dynastic proportions. William Farmer of *Claines*, Darling Point, had Anthony Hordern as neighbour in *Retford Hall*. There were the Samuel Horderns in *Babworth House*, the Lloyd-Jones in *Rosemont*, Fred Lassetter in *Redleaf*, the T. S. Morts in *Greenoaks* and the Mark Foys in *Euemmering* on Bellevue Hill. With the same merchants came the brewers who have left us quite remarkable symbols of their economic achievement. Between them the Tooths and the Reschs provided both *Cranbrook* and *Swifts*. From the 1830s *Rose Bay Lodge* — that marvellous reminder of how a colonial 'seat' could be established — to establishments such as *The Hermitage*, *Carrara*, *Trahlee* and *Ginahgulla*, we can recognise the social and cultural aspirations of the elite amongst 19th century Australians. The material in this book reinforces this recognition. Importantly, it also suggests to us what changes were wrought as a result of the sea change between Homeland and Colony.

An alternative view of the reality which is Woollahra is also apparent in the following pages. For every grand statement there have been many modest yet equally important contributions to environmental change. Woollahra's present is just as much a function of these as it is of the more renowned. The fishermen's enclave of Watsons Bay, the random cluster of buildings straddling young Oxford Street, a gin factory turned into a tannery, the infant public transport system for the region, its schools, its water supply, its amusements and the market gardens of Rose Bay can all remind us of the complex needs of suburban growth as populations treble and more than treble again over the space of two hundred years. They remind us too of the people who have serviced these needs. In this respect the photograph can be of superlative documentary importance. The collection herein certainly illustrates the point.

In *Impressions of Woollahra Past and Present* the total exceeds the sum of the parts. Taken as a whole, we are able to recognise a locality of great beauty and great achievement. A quantity of real heritage worth has already been lost in Woollahra. Those who read this book may realise that what we still have deserves our vigilance and our care. It is worth keeping.

Max Kelly
President, National Trust of Australia (NSW)

Woollahra Reflected: 18th and 19th Century Paintings and Drawings

Candice Bruce & Anita Callaway

Woollahra Reflected: 18th and 19th Century Paintings and Drawings

WHEN CAPTAIN WATKIN TENCH arrived in Port Jackson with the First Fleet he described the area east of Sydney Cove as 'exceedingly rocky, sandy and barren'. Much of the area was swamp, with steep cliffs rising behind; a topographical fact making road building an expensive and hazardous business. These factors, when combined with the pattern of land grants to the first European settlers, resulted in the most easterly points of what is now the Municipality of Woollahra, Watsons Bay and Vaucluse, being settled before those less accessible areas nearer Sydney Cove. In that early period of European settlement sites were often chosen for their pictur-esque and prominent locations, and sometimes for their isolation as in the case of Sir Henry Browne Hayes. A gentleman convict, he was transported for the abduction of an heiress in his native Ireland and being spurned by polite society, built *Vaucluse House* in 1803 (then only approachable by water) on a slope looking back towards the harbour.

Topographical painting, the depiction of towns or places of settlement, was the dominant style of colonial painting at this time. Thus, although the military government commissioned numerous artists to show the growth of the European settlement of Port Jackson from its earliest days, only a limited number of views of the eastern suburbs exist from this period, except for images of the Signal Station and the Lighthouse at South Head. Fine buildings were rare, and the vegetation generally was felt to be without interest. Land holdings were large, hence there were few in a position to offer patronage.

Captain John Piper, whose grant included all of present Point Piper and Rose Bay, commissioned Richard Read junior to depict an elegant garden party outside his house *Henrietta Villa*, and Augustus Earle to paint portraits of himself and his wife and family but these are rare images. Other nearby residents — Sir Henry Browne Hayes, the Wentworths, the Dumaresqs and the Daniel Coopers — rarely commissioned work of this standard. As if producing its own momentum, many images of *Henrietta Villa* now exist, while few of *Vaucluse House* are known, least of all any depicting Wentworth's lavish celebration of the departure of the reviled Governor Darling in 1831 when an illumination reading 'Down with the T-yr-t' lit up the night skies. Even later landowners such as Thomas Sutcliffe Mort and Thomas Ware Smart, despite building grand houses complete with their own art galleries, are not known to have commissioned works of themselves, their families, their houses or the views from them. The small watercolour which exists of Smart's house, *Mona*, is crude and sketchy, albeit interesting.

Painting remained a financially difficult profession. Augustus Earle who spent two years in New South Wales continued on his travels around the world; Richard Read struggled to survive as an artist; and Conrad Martens supported himself and his family by working as assistant librarian at the New South Wales Parliamentary Library. Martens' Romantic treatment of the landscape coupled with his prodigious output has produced a formidable quantity of views of Sydney and its environs. Less well-known are his drawings of rock and cloud formations, such as *Rocks in Double Bay*, which provided the basis for his Turneresque treatments.

Art remained the exclusive preserve of an elite group at least until the depression of the 1840s. The members of this moneyed class sought within colonial society a level of respectability probably denied them in Britain. Unsure in matters of taste, they erred on the side of conservatism. Apart from the commissions which Martens managed to secure, the landholders of Woollahra preferred importing poor copies of mediocre European art to commissioning local artists to paint local views.

This resulted in a lack of paintings of Woollahra commensurate with the size and splendour of its estates.

This early manifestation of the 'cultural cringe' also meant that there was no local support for artistic innovation. Artists, to please their clientele, persisted with the hackneyed formulae of picturesque topography. The most extreme example, perhaps, was the work of the convict George Peacock who was not a professional artist. Originally an attorney, he was transported for forgery in 1837 and was employed as a meteorologist at South Head from 1839 until the weather station closed in 1856. He painted ostensibly as a hobby, for relaxation; yet he adhered in his painting to a stifling system of self-imposed restrictions, often forcing his naturally broad brushstrokes into a finished work of postcard dimensions and obsessively painting the same view over and over. His many paintings of the scenery between South Head and Sydney Cove have a distinctly disturbed quality as a result.

With the economic upsurge which followed the gold rush of the 1850s, however, a prosperous new middle class emerged. Its members were not tied to the colonial past, but instead had a sense of separate Australian identity. Untutored in matters of taste, they were brash enough not to let that concern them. They demanded and received art which suited their egalitarian mood. As members of a new society they were possibly unaware of the European tradition in formal landscape painting of harking back to a classical mythological past, and would have thought it irrelevant had they known of it in any case. Instead, they preferred local and contemporary subjects which reflected their own informal and sentimental tastes. Artists like S. T. Gill confirmed their popularity with this market by defying the established hierarchies of art practice. Thus, Gill's watercolour of *South Head, Looking North*, in which a figure in modern dress almost leaps out of the picture to point out the melodramatic subject to the viewer, popularises and even parodies an otherwise conventionally sublime view.

Less ambitious artists chose less sensational subjects, simply painting and sketching the local scenery for their own pleasure. John Hardwick, an unemployed storekeeper who lodged at a friend's house in Paddington during 1853 and 1854, sketched his own idiosyncratic views of the area. George Roberts, another resident of Paddington who worked as a scene painter at the Royal Victoria Theatre, then in Pitt Street, Sydney, painted naive watercolour views of the district. Neither of these artists produced work which offered a challenge to an unsophisticated audience. Nor did they feel it necessary to apologize for any lack of polish in their work; it certainly proved no bar to Hardwick's selling his sketches for publication in the *Illustrated Sydney News*.

The development of lithography and the illustrated press both created and catered for the popular market by reducing the cost and increasing the circulation of works of art. Professional artists like F. C. Terry and S. T. Gill drew and painted views for the express purpose of mass-producing them as lithographs in such books as *The Australian Keepsake* and *The Australian Sketch-Book* respectively. Views of the Woollahra district, especially those taken from the scenic route along the (Old) South Head Road, were common. Lithographs were also issued to commemorate specific events which caught the imagination of the whole community, such as those by Edmund Thomas showing the wreck of the *Dunbar* at the Gap. Whereas in the past prints had been collected for their romantic associations or for their depiction of some topographical novelty, in the 1850s and 1860s they were prized for their illustration of familiar views, much as postcards were later in the century.

The subject the urban middle classes most wanted to see depicted in the art they bought was — themselves. They not only wanted pictures of familiar scenery or events, they wanted them peopled with figures after their own image. Gone were the miniscule stock figures of the landscapes of the past; in their place were active figures in modern dress for whom the landscape merely acted as a foil. Montagu Scott's painting *A Day's Picnic at Clark Island*, showing free-and-easy behaviour at an outdoor party, proved so popular that it was reproduced as a supplement in the *Illustrated Sydney News* accompanied by an extensive commentary. Similar images of Woollahra residents and visitors at work and at play were common in the illustrated papers until the end of the century.

Early in the 19th century the beauty and character of Woollahra could be experienced only by its few residents and occasional Sunday visitors. Later the subdivisions of large estates and the introduction of public transport and improved roads opened up the area to more people. Pictorial representations of Woollahra progressed from the earliest scientific records, through romantic views, to the more matter-of-fact illustrations of a comfortable and prosperous suburban way of life. Thus as the Woollahra region changed from open lands to big estates to residential areas, so did the nature of its images.

Entrance of Port Jackson · 27 January 1788.

**Entrance of Port Jackson,
27 January 1788**
WILLIAM BRADLEY
Watercolour
Mitchell Library

Bradley, first lieutenant in the
Sirius, recorded the entry of the
ships of the First Fleet into the
harbour which Captain Phillip
called 'the finest in the world, in
which a thousand sail of the line
may ride in the most perfect
security'. Port Jackson is better
known today as Sydney Harbour.

South Head and Light House, Port Jackson, N.S.Wales, with the approach of a Southerly Squall c. 1825
AUGUSTUS EARLE

Watercolour
Rex Nan Kivell Collection,
National Library of Australia

The first white Australians huddled together at Sydney Cove on the fringe of an apparently inhospitable land. Ships were their only link with the world they knew and understood. A signal flagstaff was erected on South Head in 1790; a bonfire was lit from 1793; and a lighthouse was built in 1817. Earle emphasized the colony's dependence on shipping for its news and supplies in this painting of the lighthouse as an almost celestial beacon promising safe harbour to the tiny ship tossed by stormy seas.

6

7

**The Gap, South Head
N.S.W. 1857**
EDMUND THOMAS

Watercolour
Dixson Galleries

Visits to South Head were popular
throughout the 19th century.
Staring down the sheer cliffs at the
Gap, day-trippers could combine
the current taste for sublime, awe-
inspiring views with the *frisson* of
flirting with danger. Artists
provided similar sensations at
second hand with their paintings of
the Gap, especially after the wreck
of the *Dunbar* on 20 August 1857.
Thomas painted a typically sublime
view of the disaster: the elements
are on a grander scale than the
helpless figures who, like the
viewers of the painting, bear
witness to the cruel whims of
nature. This picture was so popular
at the time that at least two versions
of it were published as lithographs.

South Head looking North c.1857

South Head looking North

South Head looking North c.1857
S. T. GILL

Watercolour
Mitchell Library

Gill, a more popularist artist who delighted in breaking artistic conventions, introduced a more human and humane response to the sublimity of the Gap with the nattily-dressed figure in the left of the picture turning in mute appeal to us, the viewers.

Sydney Heads 1865
Eugen von Guérard

Oil, bequest of Major
H. W. Hall 1974
Art Gallery of New South Wales

A track was cleared to South Head in 1803; a road (now Old South Head Road) was built by public subscription along the ridge running between the settlement at Sydney Cove and South Head in 1811; New South Head Road was completed in the 1840s. The round trip to South Head became popular with day-trippers of all classes. In von Guérard's painting, the smart carriage in the foreground shares the road with the foot-slogger in the right of the picture. Behind them stretches a landscape reminiscent of European parkland; beyond that again, the tranquil waters of the harbour. This view, often repeated by other artists as well as by von Guérard, became a standard 19th century Australian image.

North Head, Port Jackson, N.S.Wales c.1842
H. I. CAMPBELL

Watercolour
Mitchell Library

Campbell's view over the Heads from the South Head Road lacks the grandeur of von Guérard's vision; instead, he has produced a fairly realistic, if clumsily executed, topographical view. He has introduced, however, some picturesque elements into the foreground: the aboriginal family to the right, and the rustic group (with an extremely personable dog) to the left.

Colony at the South Head, Sydney, NSW c.1853
JOHN HARDWICK

Wash drawing
Mitchell Library

The earliest settlement in present-day Woollahra was the community of fishermen, pilots and signalmen at Watsons Bay. The land between South Head and Sydney Cove was not quickly developed, so for some time the village remained the peaceful retreat suggested in Hardwick's sketch. This isolation did not last, however. An intermittent ferry service called at the jetty built out into the bay from May 1854 and from the 1860s steam ferries regularly brought crowds of jaded city dwellers to Watsons Bay for a refreshing Sunday outing.

Colony at the South Head.
Sydney - NSW.

Watsons Bay, Port Jackson, Undated
S. T. GILL

Watercolour
Dixson Galleries

13

Watsons Bay, Undated
F. C. TERRY

Watercolour
Dixson Galleries

**Old Fisherman's Hut,
Vaucluse 1880
D. J.**

Oil
Mitchell Library

By 1880, a confident economy had prompted Sydney's urban sprawl and the extension of its suburbs into surrounding districts like Woollahra. Artists like the otherwise unidentified 'D. J.' reacted to the pace of development by harking back to a simpler, though imaginary, way of life. D. J.'s painting of the top-hatted fisherman happily pottering between his boat and cottage is a romantic version of what was probably in reality a fairly harsh existence.

Sydney Harbour, looking towards Sydney 1848
JACOB JANSSEN
Oil
Mitchell Library

In the 1840s, there were only a few wealthy Sydney residents who could afford to commission or buy major works from professional artists. Many of these potential patrons built grand houses on grand estates in the Woollahra district. Janssen probably aimed this pair of paintings, which together present a splendid panorama of the harbour, at such a clientele. The elegant figures dressed in the height of fashion and the landscape 'improved' in the European manner would have appealed to the taste of the smug *nouveaux riches* of the time. Even the swagman introduces no sense of discord into the idyllic scene; he seems an antipodean participant in a Dick Whittington masquerade.

Vaucluse, looking towards the Heads 1848
JACOB JANSSEN

Oil
Mitchell Library

**Vaucluse Bay, Port Jackson
1820**
JAMES WALLIS

Engraved by Walter Preston in
Wallis' *An Historical Account of
the Colony of New South Wales*
Mitchell Library

Captain Wallis of the 46th
Regiment drew several views of
New South Wales with the intention
of issuing them as engravings for
sale to the public. While
commander of the penal settlement
at Newcastle, Wallis made use of
the services of the convict Walter
Preston to engrave the copper
plates. The engraved views were
advertised in Sydney in 1819, but
Wallis took the plates back to
England with him, where they were
published in book form in 1821. In
the text which accompanied this
plate, Wallis drew attention to
'Vaucluse, a romantic Villa'. This
was the house originally built by Sir
Henry Browne Hayes, later
occupied by Lieutenant-Governor
O'Connell and, at the time of
publication of this view,
by Captain Piper.

Hall, *Vaucluse* **1869**
REBECCA MARTENS
Pencil
Dixson Library

Vaucluse House was bought by William Charles Wentworth in 1827. He found it 'a very uncomfortable residence' and soon set about improving it. To complement the picturesque features and romantic associations of the estate he commenced extensions in the Gothic Revival style, although the project was never completed. Rebecca Martens, daughter and pupil of Conrad Martens, sketched the interior of the hall with its pointed archway and Gothic furniture, providing an unusually intimate glimpse of 19th century domestic arrangements.

**Rose Bay, from Cranbrook,
Bellevue Hill, Undated**
E. B. BOULTON

Watercolour
Mitchell Library

Boulton divided his time between
his country property and Darling
Point. His vista over Rose Bay from
the slopes of Bellevue Hill is
extraordinarily detailed. Indeed, its
primary purpose would seem to
have been the recording of factual
information. The strip of fertile land
behind the bay has been cleared
and replanted, but the surrounding
slopes and promontories are still
covered with virgin bushland.

The Sacred Heart Convent, Rose Bay 1898
TOM ROBERTS

Oil on wood panel
Private collection

In this view, painted late in the 19th century, Roberts was not concerned with the need for detailed accuracy which so preoccupied earlier landscapists. Nevertheless, Horbury Hunt's neo-Gothic building can be readily identified.

The Cottage, Rose Bay 1857
CONRAD MARTENS

Watercolour, gouache, varnish
on cardboard
Australian National Gallery

Martens, an acknowledged master
of the romantic landscape, painted
this view of *The Cottage*, Rose Bay,
(also known as *Rose Bay Lodge*),
which was designed by the
architect, John Verge, in 1834 for
James Holt. It was later the home of
Daniel Cooper, the first speaker of
the Legislative Assembly who
became Sir Daniel Cooper, 1st
Baronet of Woollahra. Though
heavily disguised, it still stands in
Salisbury Road, near New South
Head Road. The building, bathed in
sunlight and framed in the
picturesque manner by
complementary dark clumps of
foliage, is the focus of attention.

Cover design for *The Rose Bay Quadrilles* 1856
EDMUND THOMAS

Engraving
Private collection

Thomas designed this charmingly rustic view of Rose Bay and *Rose Bay Lodge* and its pine trees, for the cover of the sheet music composed by William Stanley. The music may have been commissioned by Daniel Cooper to celebrate the laying of the foundation stone of *Woollahra House* on 15 December 1856.

24

Henrietta Villa 1820
RICHARD READ JUNIOR

Watercolour
Dixson Galleries

Inspired perhaps by Macquarie's
vision of New South Wales as a
permanent settlement rather than a
penal colony, Captain John Piper
built an elegant neo-classical villa
on the promontory which bears his
name. Here he attempted to
recreate the life of a British
gentleman. *Henrietta Villa* was the
setting for garden parties and balls,
as well as the family home. This
lavish lifestyle, however, resulted in
Piper's bankruptcy in 1827, forcing
the sale of this estate.

**Mrs Piper and her
Children c.1826**
AUGUSTUS EARLE

Oil
Mitchell Library

Ball at *Henrietta Villa*, Undated
FREDERICK GARLING (attrib.)

Watercolour
Private collection

**A Day's Picnic on Clark
Island 1870**
MONTAGU SCOTT

Oil on canvas
Mitchell Library, on loan to
Vaucluse House

This painting is one of few which
give us an insight into the manners
and morals of polite society in
Sydney in the late 19th century,
with one popular journal
speculating on the number of
discreet flirtations being conducted
under watchful parental eyes.

***Ginahgulla*, Bellevue Hill 1865**
F. C. TERRY

Watercolour
Mitchell Library

Terry's view of the harbour sweeps
across the Fairfax home, *Ginahgulla*,
from the crest of Bellevue Hill.
This vista was so admired that, in
1820, Macquarie changed the name
from 'Vinegar Hill' to 'Belle Vue'.

Port Jackson, New South Wales, View in Double Bay south side. Middle Head in the distance 1847
GEORGE PEACOCK

Oil
Mitchell Library

Governor Macquarie set aside 21 acres of land at Double Bay as the site of the first Botanical Gardens. When Governor Brisbane chose the Domain instead, Double Bay was surveyed by Sir Thomas Mitchell as a government village. The venture failed however, and the land was leased out for market gardens.

Rocks in Double Bay, Undated
CONRAD MARTENS

Watercolour
Dixson Library

In the 1850s a hermit known as
'Old Waterloo' lived in the caves at
Double Bay. 'A quiet, well-behaved
old man, much liked by the gentry',
he supported himself by making
brooms. Becoming a celebrity
during his lifetime, he had his
portrait painted by the artist Henry
Robinson Smith.

30

Double Bay from the Cliffs below the Church Promontory 1853
JOHN HARDWICK

Pencil
Mitchell Library

When Hardwick drew this scene, Double Bay was still largely unsettled, consisting mainly of fishermen's huts and market gardens. The house on the far right is *Jueilia* (or *Tueilia*) which Hardwick describes as 'the house built for Mrs Cooper when she was invalided'.

Hardwick notes on the right 'Road thro the wood to Rose Bay & South Head' and 'Rose Bay behind the opposite Point South Head. Cliffs & Lighthouse in distance'.

View of Darling Point from Clark Island showing *Carthona* and *Lindesay* c.1850
HENRY CURZON ALLPORT

Watercolour
Mitchell Library

In 1841 Sir Thomas Mitchell, Surveyor General of New South Wales, bought the villa *Lindesay* at the end of Darling Point so that he could supervise the building of *Carthona*, a richly decorated Gothic house at the water's edge. Mitchell had chosen the design from a pattern book by John Claudius Loudon and its style and setting were strongly reminiscent of his native Scotland. Allport's depiction, with soft foreground foliage and rippling reflections, was suitably Picturesque for contemporary taste.

View of the Bay and Lighthouse 1833
CHARLES RODIUS

Pencil
Mitchell Library

Looking east over the harbour with the Heads and the Lighthouse on the horizon, the artist has given his sweeping view a picturesque quality by the use of a rustic wooden fence and cows in the foreground.

Glenrock, Undated
J. F. MANN

Pencil
Mitchell Library

In the 1840s Thomas Whistler
Smith built the Gothic-style *Dower
House* for his widowed mother,
Penelope Smith, née Whistler. The
building, now part of Ascham
School, Darling Point, has had few
external changes. After the death of
Mrs Smith in 1866, the *Dower
House* was rented for one hundred
pounds a year to J. F. Mann, who
married the daughter of Sir Thomas
Mitchell.

Church and Villa near Double Bay, NSW 1853

Church and Villa near Double Bay, NSW 1853
JOHN HARDWICK
Pencil
Mitchell Library

Darling Point Road winding past the entrance gates of *Mona* (on the left above the woman and child) to St. Marks Church on the crest of Darling Point. Hardwick notes 'Spire unfinished but the second stage is octagon shaped. My supplement's bad'. Hardwick had anticipated the later completion of the spire in this sketch.

***Mona*, Darling Point, Sydney, NSW 1844**
SAMUEL PROUT HILL

Watercolour
Mitchell Library

Thomas Ware Smart's house *Mona* overlooking Rushcutters Bay was built on fifteen acres originally granted to James Dunlop, the government astronomer, in 1835 'for one residence only, buildings to be erected to the value and cost of one thousand pounds'.

The strange humps in the foreground were possibly cloches used for growing vegetables, as Smart was known to have surrounded his house with extensive market gardens. Although Smart built an art gallery at *Mona* which he filled with European paintings and opened to the public on occasion, he is not known to have commissioned a painting of the house, and this simple sketch is the only known view of the estate.

**The Water Famine in the
Sydney Suburbs —
Moonlight Scene in Woollahra**
ARTHUR COLLINGRIDGE

Woodcut
Illustrated Sydney News,
4 September, 1880

Fresh water had always been in
short supply in Woollahra, and
later development in the region
exacerbated the problem. Although
in 1878 residents of Paddington
were promised reticulated water
from the Waverley Reservoir, by
1880 this supply was still not
available.

1, Paddington Bus 1857
THOMAS TYRWITT BALCOMBE

Pen and ink
Dixson Galleries

The omnibus was the principal means of transport to Paddington until replaced by the steam train in 1881. 'As instruments of torture the rack was mild and humane compared with a Sydney omnibus in the 'fifties. They were narrow and low with straight sides and a piece of board not much more than six inches wide along each of the seats'. Gill's depiction of a 'bone-rattler' is contrasted with a genteel horse and buggy.

**Watsons Bay and North Head
from the South Head Road
c.1858
S. T. GILL**

Watercolour
Mitchell Library

**View from Mill Hill Estate
looking North, 1892**
UNKNOWN

Engraving
Real estate advertisement,
Mitchell Library

40

Oxford Street, Paddington,
looking west from Point
Piper Road, Undated
UNKNOWN

Engraving
Mitchell Library

Quarry in Paddington Wood 1853
JOHN HARDWICK
Pencil
Mitchell Library

Paddington was rich in a particularly high quality sandstone and had many quarries. This quarry was situated near Underwood's Paddock and was commonly used as a short cut to Rushcutters Bay. Goats and cows wandered randomly throughout the area, frequently bringing bitter complaints from residents.

Point Piper's Road 1861
GEORGE ROBERTS

Watercolour
Dixson Library

Captain (or Point Piper/s) Road (now Jersey Road) was a rough track leading down to Point Piper and Rose Bay from Paddington, and was the main road into that area during the 1830s and 1840s.

Roberts married a member of the Gordon family which was amongst the first to settle in Paddington, and has perhaps depicted himself in the foreground of this painting, sketching the scene before him.

The Cascade, Paddington 1859
GEORGE ROBERTS

Watercolour
Mitchell Library

The use of diminutive figures set
against the landscape was a
common device in 19th century
landscape painting and was meant
to provoke in the viewer feelings of
awe at Nature's grandeur. The
waterfall depicted was diverted to
create Cascade Street.

Glenmore Tannery 1861
GEORGE ROBERTS
Watercolour
Mitchell Library

Cooper and Underwood's distillery was sold in 1860 to James Begg who converted it into a tannery. It operated as such for more than 40 years and, along with a brewery and a dairy, was part of the early commercial life of Paddington. Roberts has softened his drawing by the use of foliage to 'frame' his page.

Lower Paddington from Darlinghurst Windmill 1853
JOHN HARDWICK

Pencil
Mitchell Library

Hardwick lived in Paddington for three years in the early 1850s when it was principally a collection of workers' cottages surrounding the Victoria Barracks. Most residents were stonemasons who worked locally in the many quarries with which Paddington abounded.

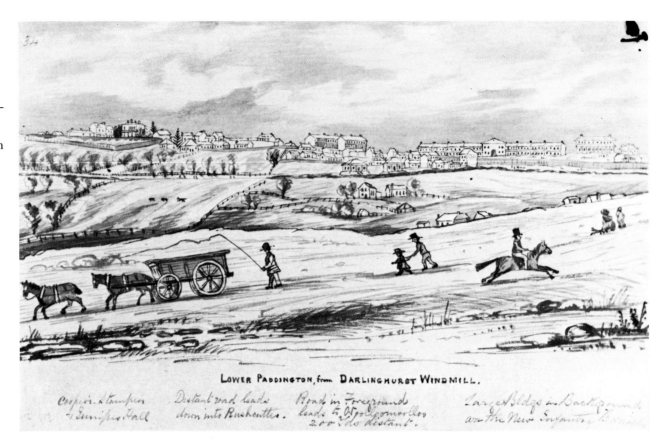

LOWER PADDINGTON, from DARLINGHURST WINDMILL.

Coopers & tampers
& Juniper Hall

Distant road leads
down into Rushcutters.

Road in Foreground
leads to Woolloomooloo
200 yds distant.

Large Bldgs in Background
are the New Infantry Barracks

Panorama of Paddington 1853
JOHN HARDWICK

Watercolour
Mitchell Library

Most of Hardwick's drawings were intended for relatives back in England and carry lengthy inscriptions identifying buildings.

The top drawing shows Gordon's Mill, the Blue Mountains in the distance and the Victoria Barracks.

The bottom drawing shows the junction of (Old) South Head Road and Point Piper Road (now Oxford Street and Jersey Road), 'the Scotch Chapel, *Juniper Hall*, Stamper & Cooper's, Tempest's House, Perry's House and *Villa House*.'

View of Sydney Harbour 1861
GEORGE ROBERTS

Watercolour
Mitchell Library

These two panoramas give slightly differing views of the harbour looking north-east. While neither artist was trained, both works give accurate and detailed information on the area depicted and constantly delight with their freshness and naivete. Hardwick has drawn 'Mr. Cooper's wallend' on the left; in the centre the two buildings of *Mona Terrace* with *Mona* and St. Marks above and 'the sea peeping behind'; on the right 'New South Head Road disappearing in Double Bay'.

Rushcutters Bay and the waters of Port Jackson from Mr Stamper's Back Door 1853

Rushcutters Bay and the
waters of Port Jackson
from Mr Stamper's Back
Door 1853
JOHN HARDWICK

Pencil
Mitchell Library

View of the Coopers' Residence c.1853
John Hardwick

Pencil
Mitchell Library

A view of *Ormond Lodge*, parts of which are still standing on the east side of Underwood Street. *Ormond Lodge* was built in the grounds of *Juniper Hall*, and became Cooper's residence in the 1840s, after he had lost his money in the depression and had leased *Juniper Hall/ Ormond House* as the Asylum for Destitute Children. Robert Cooper, the distiller, named his house *Juniper Hall* after the berries which give its gin its flavour. When Judge Kinchela leased it in the 1830s, he gave it the name of *Ormond House* in an attempt to escape the association with distilleries. Used as an orphanage, an institution for delinquent children and a ladies' seminary over the years, it is still a landmark of Paddington and has been restored by the National Trust of Australia (NSW) for the Bicentenary. On the left, Hardwick has written 'Palings dividing the grounds after the hall from ours. It was all in Cooper's palmy days'.

**The Gap, South Head,
Sydney Harbour 1895**
B. E. MINNS

Watercolour
Private collection

Crowds of visitors still came to
South Head at the end of the 19th
century much as they had since the
road was opened in 1811. As Minns
shows, however, they were now
more interested in the fashionable
spectacle they themselves created
than in the view itself.

Woollahra in Camera:
Photographs and Postcards

Julian Holland

Postcard commentary and captions in association
with Anthony Maher

Woollahra in Camera:
Photographs and Postcards

THE MID-19TH CENTURY saw a rapid growth in Australia's population, partly as a result of the discovery of gold. The recently developed art of photography quickly established itself among the commercial activities of the cities and towns. Photographic portraits could be obtained in a fraction of the time and for a fraction of the cost of a painted portrait. Photographs of family members could be sent to relatives 'at home' in England. Sydney's rapidly changing landscape also was soon captured and preserved by the new technology — the record of the artist's brush and palette was complemented by the monochrome images of the wet-plate camera.

The early photographic techniques — the daguerreotype, the ambrotype and wet-plate glass negatives — required considerable equipment and technical skill, not suited to widespread amateur activity. Yet in Sydney in the 1850s a remarkable number of amateur photographers were recording streetscapes, domestic views or picturesque bushland scenes — there were perhaps 30 or more of these amateurs! However, it was not until the coming of the dry-plate technique, and then the roll film and cheap cameras in the very last years of the 19th century that photography was opened up as a popular hobby — the era of the snapshot began on the eve of Federation. For the most part then the early images of Sydney were taken by professional photographers.

Today the photographic image is everywhere. A tourist brochure without enticing photographs would not attract many holidaymakers. The power of photographs to capture the imagination with an immediacy greater than words was realised very early. The Great Exposition held in London in 1851 was a showcase for the new cornucopia of arts and products manufactured after the industrial revolution. Popular interest in photography was greatly increased as a result of the daguerreotypes and calotypes on exhibit. Even so the jurors expressed disappointment at the absence of examples of many possible uses for photography, noting, among other things, that there were 'no delineations of tropical or remote scenery'.

While American daguerreotypists were praised for the technical excellence of their works, photography in Australia was barely established in 1851. In the many succeeding exhibitions in the 19th century, however, photography had an established place and the Australian colonies used the medium — paper prints from glass-plate negatives — to promote themselves with pictures showing the progress of civilisation in the new country and the many attractions of its scenery.

Intercolonial exhibitions were held in several of the colonial capitals. The New South Wales Government Printing Office's collection of glass-plate negatives dates back to the commissioning of a commercial portrait photographer, Charles Pickering, to prepare an album of photographs relating to the second Metropolitan Intercolonial Exhibition in 1870. Subsequently Pickering supplied views of Sydney for the London Exhibition of 1873. It was not long before the Government Printing Office employed several photographers. A few photographs from this magnificent collection are included in the following pages, including the impressive picture of the Macquarie Lighthouse and its successor.

It was not only the colonial governments who perceived the value of showing Australian photographs at international exhibitions abroad. A German immigrant, Bernard Holtermann, had a remarkable vision. Having made a fortune in gold mining near Hill End, Holtermann was inspired to embark on a project of photographic documentation by the arrival of the itinerant photographer Beaufoy Merlin and his young assistant Charles Bayliss.

Holtermann erected a gentleman's residence in North Sydney which included a tower specially designed for taking panoramic views of Sydney Harbour. The largest of these panoramas was 33 feet (10 metres) long, made from a series of very large wet-plate glass negatives. Holtermann claimed to have produced the largest photographic views in the world, and soon he was to set off to impress the world with pictures of his adopted home. The panorama formed the centrepiece of a display of New South Wales photographs Holtermann took first to the Centennial Exhibition in Philadelphia in 1876 and then on to the Exposition Universelle International in Paris two years later. As he afterwards expressed himself in a parliamentary address, Holtermann believed that the display in European galleries of photographs of Sydney, 'its public buildings, streets and other architecture, also of the most important public buildings and public works throughout the colony' would excite the attention of the most desirable class of immigrant.

Merlin, who had been appointed 'Photographic Artist of the Holtermann Exhibition' at the end of 1872, became further convinced of the need for such a travelling display when he read of the failure of New South Wales to be represented at the Vienna International Exhibition in 1873. Merlin had completed a photographic tour of country towns as well as assembling 200 negatives of Sydney when he was taken ill with a respiratory complaint and died — undoubtedly a consequence in part of his many years of exposure to dangerous photographic chemicals. His assistant Bayliss continued with the project. Several of the negatives in the surviving Holtermann Collection, now in the Mitchell Library, show different aspects of Woollahra; despite the passage of more than a 100 years, many of the scenes are instantly recognisable.

Landscape photographs were sold in series or individually as well as being shown in exhibitions. Some photographic studios sold sets by subscription, others prepared albums of views. Such albums were often presented to local or visiting dignitaries, or taken by prominent citizens for presentation when travelling abroad. These photographs were produced directly from the glass negatives. The introduction of techniques for mass-producing photographic images led to their use in illustrated papers and magazines in place of engravings hand copied from photographs.

The first years of European settlement in Australia had been concerned with surviving in an alien landscape. By the Centenary, in 1888, many well established towns and cities were inhabited by third and fourth generation Australians, plans for federation of the colonies were advancing and the landscape was seen with more sympathetic eyes. The development of dry-plate glass negatives — not requiring on-the-spot preparation and development — enabled photographers to explore the beauty of Australia's wilderness with much greater freedom. Just as the writings of Henry Lawson and Banjo Patterson bolstered the rural myth for a principally urban population, so did the works of photographers like John Paine and John W. Lindt. It is significant that the Royal National Park (23 kilometres south of Sydney), founded in 1879, was only the second National Park in the world after Yellowstone in the United States. This celebration of landscape was not limited to the wilderness. Sydney's harbour with its points and bays presents endless opportunity to the photographer, but was probably never more beautiful as an urban setting than in the early years of this century when the buildings were in harmony with the contours of the landscape.

The boom in postcards which began at the end of the 19th century was also a product of technological developments. Although the postcard is still with us, it has never regained the popularity it held before the First World War. Looking at old postcards today we can glimpse a world long gone and yet still within the memory of older people, a world where the transport and communications we take for granted were almost non-existent. Postcards show streets where trams were the main form of transport and cars were a rarity. Few people had telephones before the

First World War and postcards themselves were often used to send short messages. At Federation, postal and telegraphic services were taken over by the Australian government, but the former colonial authorities continued to operate with considerable autonomy. It was only a decade after Federation that Australian stamps replaced those of the different states. The postage stamps suggest a world of stability, without the rapid spiral of inflation which daily confronts us. A postcard could be sent to London before the First World War for one penny. This had increased to a penny halfpenny in the Depression years and doubled to threepence by the mid-1950s.

The quality of the early postcards varied considerably. Some were direct prints, but these were generally cards with small production runs. Postcards of news events such as a visiting fleet, had to be produced quickly and were soon out of date. Amateur photographers could have their prints made with postcard backing. (It is no coincidence that modern snapshot prints are the shape and size of postcards.) Photomechanical processes were used for mass-produced postcards, some of the finest of which were sent to Germany for printing in the first decade of the century — a reminder of the growing technological power of a nation with which Australia would soon be at war. Although the photographic negatives were black and white, a variety of techniques — some more successful than others — were used to produce coloured postcards.

The photographic scenes were often embellished with decorative borders. Australian native flora was widely used in decorative motifs during the Federation Era and these are sometimes found on postcards. The decoration on later postcards degenerated to crudely drawn picture frames. During the heyday of the postcard they were collected with enthusiasm. Today, these same cards can still be collected quite cheaply and serve as an interesting record of the collector's locality.

Amateur photographs are the most idiosyncratic and fascinating part of our photographic heritage. A number of books, both anthologies and specialist studies, have been produced in recent years, largely drawn from the work of professional photographers. The work of amateurs is much less familiar and often still in private hands. While there are surviving photographs of Woollahra taken in the 1850s, all but a tiny fraction of non-professional photographs were taken this century.

For the purposes of this publication, the majority of photographs used are those of professionals. However, family albums containing subject matter and character differing from those of the professionals have an equally important part to play in the photographic history of the community. It is often the different aspect provided by these private views of the past which gives them their importance.

Landscape and Settlement

**Rushcutters Bay Road on
the way from Sydney to
South Head, 1877**

Photographer unknown
Mitchell Library

Edgecliff, 8 October, 1929

Photographer: HERBERT SHAW
Woollahra Library

59

**Panorama of Darling Point
from Clark Island**

Photographer unknown
Mitchell Library

Double Bay c.1885

Photographer: JOHN PAINE
Historic Photograph Collection,
University of Sydney

Double Bay, Sydney, N. S. W.

Double Bay, boats on beach

Postcard, coloured, printed in Germany
Private collection

Woollahra Point (Point Piper seen from Double Bay)

Postcards
Private collection

Rocky outcrops give way to rooftops

WOOLLAHRA POINT, SYDNEY
Nº 18

POST CARD

THE ADDRESS ONLY TO BE WRITTEN ON THIS SIDE.

¾·0

SWAIN & CO. SYDNEY. COPYRIGHT.

Miss Ivy Sherren,
Little Barongarook,
Colac
·Victoria

Rose Bay & Woolahra Point

Many thanks for p card. Will be pleased to
exchange with you. Hoping you will like this.
What kind do you prefer. Love from Hilda Dean

65

Double Bay from Point Piper

Postcard, coloured, printed
in Saxony
Private collection

1592 – Double Bay from Woollahra Pt., Sydney.

1635 – Point Piper, Sydney.

Point Piper

Postcard, coloured, printed
in Germany
Private collection

THE ROSE SERIES P. 5125
Copyright

WOOLAHRA POINT, ROSE BAY, SYDNEY, N.S.W.

Woollahra Point (Point Piper
seen from Rose Bay)
Postcard
Private collection

67

Looking across Rose Bay from Bellevue Hill

Photographer unknown
Woollahra Library

68

Chinese market gardens at Rose Bay, 1923

Labor Daily photograph
Mitchell Library

Harbour from Bellevue Hill

Postcard, published by Samuel
Wood, Sydney, printed in
Germany
Private collection

2276. The Harbour from Bellevue Hill, Sydney, N.S.W.

Parsley Bay, Vaucluse

Postcard, Swain & Co., Sydney
Private collection

Watsons Bay

One of the earliest settlements in Sydney, and long a tourist destination, Watsons Bay has been a popular subject for the photographer, amateur and professional alike, for more than a century.

Watsons Bay from Kutti Beach, c.1885

Photographer: JOHN PAINE
Historic Photograph Collection,
University of Sydney

WATSON'S BAY

**Panorama of Watsons Bay
c.1875**

Holtermann Collection,
Mitchell Library

At Watsons Bay looking up the
Harbour c.1880
Photographer: Attributed to
ALEXANDER BRODIE
Historic Photograph Collection,
University of Sydney

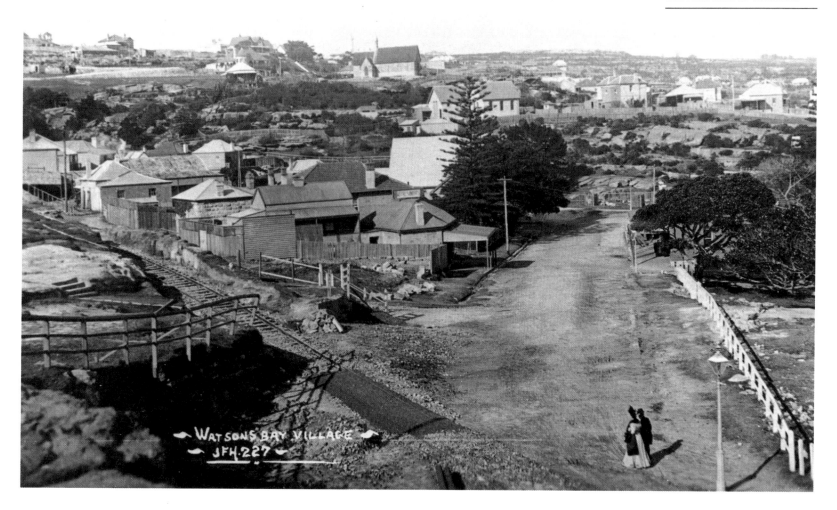

Watsons Bay village,
Postcard
Photographer: FRANK HURLEY
The Josef Lebovic Collection

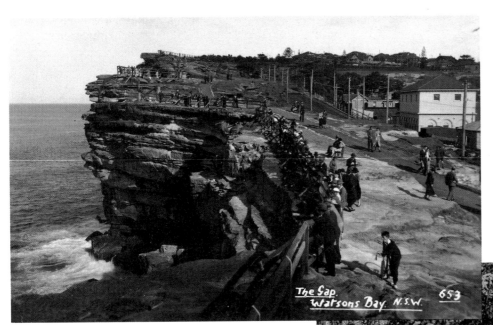

The Gap (Watsons Bay)

Postcard
Private collection

The Gap.
Watsons Bay. N.S.W. 653

Watsons Bay

Postcard, Swain & Co., Sydney
Private collection

Watson's Bay, Sydney N.S.W.

27. *Beach, Watson's Bay. N.S.W. (Showing Military Reserve)* "Carlton" Series D'hurst Copyright.

Watsons Bay showing military reserve

Postcard
Private collection

Hauling in at Watsons Bay
Photographer unknown
Mitchell Library

Looking up the Harbour from Watsons Bay c.1885

Photographer: JOHN PAINE
Historic Photograph Collection,
University of Sydney

The Marine Biological Station on Green (or Laing's) Point had been completed only a few years earlier.

Camp Cove

Postcard, colour tinted
Empire Postcard
Private collection

' 29/6/08 . . . This is one of Sydney
harbour beauty spots . . . It is a
favourite round trip to go there by
tram (1½ hours ride) & back by
ferry steamer (1½ hours)
cost 8d. ret. . . . '

COPYRIGHT.

412. WATSONS BAY FROM SOUTH HEAD.

Watzons Bay, Sydney Harbour

Summer House

Postcard, coloured, made in
Saxony for G. Giovanardi,
Sydney
Private collection

Watsons Bay.

Scenes in Sydney, Watsons Bay
Postcard, coloured, printed
in Saxony
Private collection

Buildings

Gilbey's Hut near Parsley Bay c.1895

Photographer unknown
Mitchell Library

The Municipality of Woollahra contains many historic buildings, some of them open to the public, some part of schools or other institutions. Humble pioneer dwellings such as Gilbey's Hut near Parsley Bay have long since gone. So, too, have some more substantial residences in the district, notably *Clovelly* at Watsons Bay and *Woollahra House* on Point Piper. Historic photographs are a reminder that in the short history of European settlement in Woollahra, the landscape has undergone many changes.

Sir John Robertson's home
Clovelly at Watsons Bay c.1880

Photographer unknown
Woollahra Library

The house was demolished in 1903.

**Sacred Heart Convent
School, Rose Bay**

Postcard, published by
G. Giovanardi, Sydney
Private collection

No. 31 Sacred Heart Convent, Rose Bay. N. S. W.   G. Giovanardi, Publisher, Sydney.

Sacré Coeur, Rose Bay.

Sacré Coeur, Rose Bay

Postcard, printed in Austria
Private collection

Cranbrook , State Government
House, Sydney

Postcard, coloured c.1910.
L. & H. Publishing Co.
Private collection

Since 1918, Cranbrook School.

"Cranbrook," State Government House, Sydney.

Vaucluse House , 1909

Photographer unknown
New South Wales Government
Printing Office, Australia

Vaucluse House, the home of
William Charles Wentworth and
his family, was purchased by the
New South Wales Government in
1910 and has been open to the
public since 1924.

Family Dining Room,
Vaucluse House

Photographer: THOS. J. LAWLOR
Postcard
Private collection

The Ballroom, *Vaucluse House*

Photographer: THOS. J. LAWLOR.
Postcard
Private collection

The glass display cabinets seem quaintly incongruous to modern eyes. In recent years, *Vaucluse House* and its garden have been restored to the character of a 19th century home.

Transport and Communications

Rose Bay c.1875

Holtermann Collection,
Mitchell Library

*'For many years there were
complaints about the condition
of the roads . . .'* The pines mark
the garden of *Rose Bay Lodge* .

**Horse-drawn buses at the
Ocean Street terminus c.1880**

Photographer: CHARLES BAYLISS
Mitchell Library

Edgecliff at the corner of New South
Head Road and lower Ocean Street
(now Ocean Avenue). The growing
population was served by an
expanding network of omnibus routes.

Tram in New South Head Road, Rose Bay, 1924

Labor Daily photograph
Mitchell Library

The tram service reached Dover Road, Rose Bay, in 1900 and was extended to Watsons Bay Wharf in 1909.

Kent Road, Rose Bay

Photographer unknown
Woollahra Library

An amateur postcard showing motor cars parked in Kent Road, Rose Bay, in 1920. The ruins of the clubhouse of the Royal Sydney Golf Club, which was destroyed by fire, can be seen in the background.

Sydney — Rose Bay

Thanks so much for the post card with you + the donkey on it. I am getting quite a grand collection

No. 57. L. von Koenneritz, Sydney. Photo. by Ward & Farran, Exchange Studios, Sydney.

Rose Bay

Photograph by WARD & FARREN,
Exchange Studios, Sydney
Postcard, L. von Koenneritz,
Sydney
Private collection

Double Bay

Postcard, coloured, R.J. Melb.
& Sydney, printed in Britain
Private collection

By comparison with the same
scenes today, more remarkable
than the presence of the tram cars is
the absence of motor cars.
Notable also is the spread of
'telegraph' poles indicating the
growing use of telephones.

Double Bay

Edgecliff Post and Telegraph Office c.1925, corner of New South Head Road and Ocean Street

Labor Daily photograph
Mitchell Library

The Macquarie Tower and its successor side by side in 1881
New South Wales Government Printing Office, Australia

Lying between ocean and harbour, South Head has been involved with the guidance of shipping since the early years of the colony. When the light of the Macquarie Tower (erected in 1816 on outer South Head) needed replacing, it was decided to erect a new and higher tower immediately behind the old. The new lighthouse, the first in Australia to be equipped with electric light, was brought into operation in 1883.

'Macquarie Light'
Watsons Bay - Sydney - JFH 125

Macquarie Light, Watsons Bay

Photographer: FRANK HURLEY
Postcard
Tinted photograph with embossed border showing waratah and flannel-flower motifs.

This multiple exposure of the Macquarie (or South Head) Light indicates the skill and artistic imagination which made Frank Hurley Australia's leading scenic photographer for half a century.

Sydney. South Head Lighthouse. Leuchtthurm des South Head.
Phare du South Head.

For Your Collection With love from Harry

L. von Koenneritz, Sydney. — Photo by Ward & Farran, Exchange Studios, Sydney. 69.

South Head Lighthouse

Photograph by WARD & FARREN,
Exchange Studios, Sydney
Postcard, L. von Koenneritz,
Sydney
Private collection

Hornby Light

Postcard, printed in Germany

The Hornby Light was erected on
inner South Head to improve the
safety of shipping after the *Dunbar*
was wrecked in a storm near the
Gap, Watsons Bay, in 1857, with
only one survivor.

Light House, Inner South Head, Sydney.

Pilot Steamer, *Captain Cook*

Photographed in Watsons
Bay in 1921
Postcard
New South Wales Government
Printing Office, Australia

A pilot service for incoming ships
was established at Watsons Bay not
long after the start of the Colony.
Indeed, Robert Watson, after whom
the Bay is named, was appointed
pilot and harbour master in 1811.
The pilot steamer, *Captain Cook*, the
second pilot vessel of that name,
operated from 1893 until 1939.

Flying-boat docked in Rose Bay, 1957

Photographer unknown
Historic Photograph Collection,
University of Sydney

A flying-boat service to Britain
operated from a base at Lyne Park,
Rose Bay, from 1938. In more
recent years, the flying-boats took
holiday-makers to Lord Howe
Island.

Work and Leisure

The staff of the Rose Bay
Ice Works c.1918
Photographer unknown
Woollahra Library

Class photograph, Double Bay Public School c.1910

Photographer unknown
Woollahra Library

The School began in 1883 with an enrolment of 62 pupils each paying a fee of threepence per week.

**Class photograph,
Watsons Bay School, 1919**

Photographer unknown
Woollahra Library

The bare-footed children contrast
with the well-shod pupils of Double
Bay.

Workmen at Parsley Bay
c.1910

Photographer unknown
Woollahra Library

Seven Shillings Beach, Double Bay (Redleaf Pool)

Postcard
Private collection

Sydney's harbour beaches have long been the resort of picnickers, swimmers and photographers alike. Woollahra's diverse beaches have been captured in numerous postcards.

Double Bay

Postcard, published by Samuel Wood, Sydney, printed in Saxony
Private collection

Picnic on the Beach
Photographer unknown
Woollahra Library

Yvere moored in Vaucluse Bay
c.1915

Photographer: HAROLD REID
Private collection

South Head, Sydney

Bathing, Sydney Heads.

**Bathing, Sydney Heads
Below the Hornby Light**

Postcard, Art Series, printed
in Australia
Private collection

White City Amusement Park, Rushcutters Bay c.1915

Photographer unknown
Woollahra Library

' *The park occupies a site of nearly ten acres in extent into which has been packed a miniature city, with lakes, canals, fountains, pleasure palaces, and a collection of mysteries, illusions and laughter-* *making devices selected from the best of those in vogue at similar resorts at other parts of the world .*'

White City Amusement Park operated during the summer months of 1913 to 1917.

Roller-skating instructors, White City, Rushcutters Bay, c.1915

Photographer unknown
Woollahra Library

Woollahra Park, Rose Bay
c.1930

Photographer unknown
Woollahra Library

Sydney Heads, The Entrance to Sydney Harbour

Sydney Heads, The Entrance to Sydney Harbour

Postcard, printed in Great Britain, Wattle and Southern Cross border
Private collection

Impressions of Woollahra 1988:
Bicentennial Art Contest

Impressions of Woollahra 1988:
Bicentennial Art Contest

OVER 240 ENTRIES WERE RECEIVED for the Bicentennial Art Contest which was judged by Edmund Capon, the Director of the Art Gallery of NSW.

Mr Capon selected 50 of the entries to be hung at the Holdsworth Gallery in December, 1987, and at the opening of this exhibition, he complimented the entrants on their sense of exuberance and colour, saying 'That sense of vitality — expressed in exuberance and colour — probably characterises the spirit of Woollahra municipality'. Mr Capon also commented upon the diversity of styles, and, as the artists had been allowed considerable latitude in interpreting the theme 'Impressions of Woollahra', the fact that several of the best entries had captured the spirit of the area rather than simply its physical appearance.

The wide variety of subjects and styles entered for the competition emphasised that by the 1980s the function and presentation of the artistic image had evolved to reflect the complexity and vitality of a developed society. The choice of subject and the medium of presentation is now the key to the work, and leaves more to the perceptions and emotional responses of the viewer. There is room still for the picturesque, the romantic, the witty and the almost photographic representation, as well as the opportunity for social commentary.

The winning entry by Vicky Varvaressos of Paddington, *Having coffee with Mrs Piper*, is just such a 'social' picture, in great contrast to the landscapes amongst the entries. This artist has long drawn on advertising and social stereotypes, using humour and a controlled sense of anger to portray the sense of alienation and exploitation experienced by many of her fellow citizens.

A feature of the contest was the success of women artists, who won 9 of the 10 unrestricted prizes. Nanette Basser of East Lindfield even won two prizes — second prize in the open class with her strong impressionistic acrylic *Memories*, and second prize in the works on paper class, with a charcoal drawing, *Across the Bay*.

First prize in the open section was won by Naomi Lewis of Dover Heights, for her effective gouache and pastel *Rose Bay Avenue*. The watercolour first prize went to Judith White of Seaforth, who brilliantly combined striking colour and social comment in *If Lifestyle Is A Symbol Of Success*. In the works on paper class, first prize was won by Maadi Einfeld of Vaucluse with a semi-impressionistic ink drawing, *Vaucluse Bay Dinghies*.

One of the most interesting entries came from a local artist in her 80th year, Olga Mary Anderson of Rose Bay, who won the prize for the best work by a woman senior citizen resident in Woollahra, for the acrylic *Rose Bay Late Afternoon*.

The winning paintings are in the possession of Woollahra Municipal Council and will form the nucleus of a municipal art collection.

Having Coffee With Mrs Piper
VICKI VARVARESSOS

Painting in enamels

Winner of the Grand Prize
of $25000
Privately sponsored

118

Rose Bay Avenue
NAOMI LEWIS
Gouache and Pastel

Winner of First Prize in the
Open Class, $8000
Sponsored by Australian
Bicentennial Authority and
Woollahra Municipal Council

Memories
NANETTE BASSER
Acrylic Painting

Winner of Second Prize in the
Open Class, $5000
Sponsored by Australian
Bicentennial Authority and
Woollahra Municipal Council

Paddington, 1987

LOLA LYNCH

Oil Painting

Winner of Third Prize in
Open Class, $3000
Sponsored by Australian
Bicentennial Authority and
Woollahra Municipal Council

If Lifestyle is a Symbol of Success. . .
JUDITH WHITE

Winner of First Prize in
Watercolour Class, $3000
Sponsored by Double Bay Chamber
of Commerce and its members,
Holland Fine Art and Mr Tony Little

Nielsen Park
ADA CLARK

Winner of Second Prize in
Watercolour Class, $2000
Sponsored by Double Bay Chamber
of Commerce and its members,
Holland Fine Art and Mr Tony Little

Ocean Avenue
PETER YEOMANS

Winner of Third Prize in
Watercolour Class, $1000
Sponsored by Double Bay Chamber
of Commerce and its members,
Holland Fine Art and Mr Tony Little

Vaucluse Bay Dinghies
MAADI EINFELD

Ink Drawing on Paper

Winner of First Prize in Works on
Paper Class, $3000
Sponsored by The Realty Property
Group and Mr Ray Aston, MLA for
Vaucluse.

Across the Bay
NANETTE BASSER

Charcoal

Winner of Second Prize in Works
on Paper Class, $2000
Sponsored by The Realty Property
Group and Mr Ray Aston, MLA for
Vaucluse.

126

Camp. Cove Beach, Sydney. Australia. - The first landing place of Governor Arthur Phillip, 21st January 1788
P/o. Natasha Florean 1987

Camp Cove Beach, Sydney
NATASHA FLOREAN

Screenprint

Winner of Third Prize in Works on
Paper Class, $1000
Sponsored by The Realty Property
Group and Mr Ray Aston, MLA for
Vaucluse.

127

Rose Bay, Late Afternoon
OLGA MARY ANDERSON

Acrylic Painting

Winner of a Special Prize for a
Senior Citizen Woman Artist
resident in the municipality,
$1000
Sponsored by Eastern
Suburbs Newspapers

**Paddington Houses —
Glenmore Road**
MAT MATUSCHKA
Oil Painting

Winner of a Special Prize for a
Senior Citizen Male Artist
resident in the municipality, $1000
Sponsored by Media House

129